FAR

D0770490

Early String Quartets
Op. 18 Complete

Ludwig van Beethoven

From the Breitkopf & Härtel Complete Works Edition

DOVER PUBLICATIONS, INC.
Mineola, New York

Beethoven's Complete String Quartets and the Grosse Fuge are available in Dover edition 0-486-22361-2. This full-size publication, drawn from Breitkopf & Härtel's Complete Works Edition, contains Opp. 18, 59, 74, 95, 127, 130–133, and 135.

Bibliographical Note

This Dover edition, first published in 2003, is an unabridged republication of Op. 18, Nos. 1–6, *from Serie 6, Zweiter Band: Quartette für 2 Violinen, Bratsche und Violoncell of Ludwig van Beethoven's Werke. Vollständige kritisch durchgesehene überall berechtigte Ausgabe. Mit Genehmigung aller Originalverleger*, originally published by Breitkopf & Härtel, Leipzig, n.d. The Dover edition adds a contents list and new English headings throughout.

International Standard Book Number: 0-486-43133-9

Manufactured in the United States of America
Dover Publications, Inc., 31 East 2nd Street, Mineola, N.Y. 11501

CONTENTS

The six quartets of Op. 18 were composed in 1800 and published in 1801.

String Quartet No. 1

in F Major, Op. 18, No. 1

1

Adagio affettuoso ed appassionato.

SCHERZO.

Trio.

String Quartet No. 2

in G Major, Op. 18, No. 2

Scherzo Allegro.

Scherzo D.C.

Allegro molto quasi Presto.

String Quartet No. 3

in D Major, Op. 18, No. 3

Andante con moto.

Allegro.

Minore.

String Quartet No. 4

in C Minor, Op. 18, No. 4

SCHERZO.
Andante scherzoso quasi Allegretto.

MENUETTO.
Allegretto.

Trio.

Allegro.

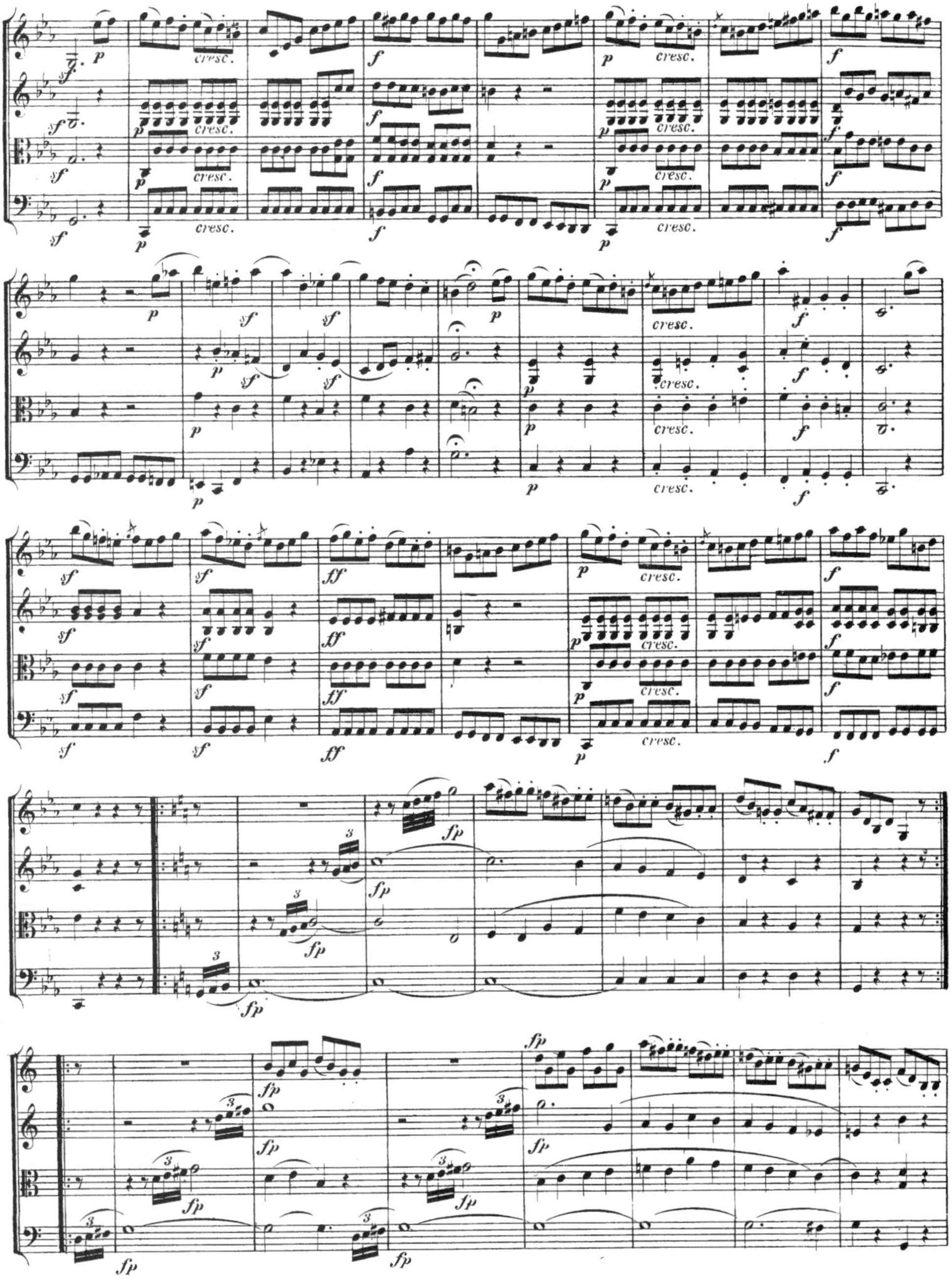

String Quartet No. 5
in A Major, Op. 18, No. 5

MENUETTO.

Var. 3.

String Quartet No. 6
in B-flat Major, Op. 18, No. 6

SCHERZO.
Allegro.

LA MALINCONIA.

Questo pezzo si deve trattare colla più gran delicatezza.